RANCHO NOTORIOUS

RANCHO NOTORIOUS

POEMS BY

Richard Garcia

American Poets Continuum Series No. 64

BOA EDITIONS, LTD. ❖ ROCHESTER, NY ❖ 2001

First Edition
00 01 02 03 7 6 5 4 3 2 1

Publications by BOA Editions, Ltd. — a not-for-profit corporation under section 501 (c) (3) of the United States Internal Revenue Code — are made possible with the assistance of grants from the Literature Program of the New York State Council on the Arts, the Literature Program of the National Endowment for the Arts, the Sonia Raiziss Giop Charitable Foundation, The Halcyon Hill Foundation, The Chase Manhattan Foundation, as well as from the Mary S. Mulligan Charitable Trust, the County of Monroe, NY, and The CIRE Foundation.

See page 104 for special individual acknowledgments.

Cover Design: Lisa Mauro / Mauro Design
Art: *Rocking Horse*, 1989, color etching and aquatint (no. 30) by Carlos
    Almaraz, Courtesy Elsa Flores Almaraz
Interior design and composition: Scribe Typography
Manufacturing: McNaughton & Gunn, Lithographers
BOA Logo: Mirko

LIBRARY OF CONGRESS CATALOGING-IN-PUBLICATION DATA

García, Richard, 1941–
    Rancho notorious: poems / by Richard Garcia. — 1st ed.
        p. cm. — (American poets continuum series; no. 64)
    ISBN 1-929918-01-1 (alk. paper)
        I. Title. II. American poets continuum series; vol. 64.

    PS3557.A71122 R3 2001
    811'.54—DC21   00-069675

BOA Editions, Ltd.
Steven Huff, Publisher
Richard Garth, Chair, Board of Directors
A. Poulin, Jr., President & Founder (1976–1996)
260 East Avenue
Rochester, NY 14604

www.boaeditions.org

NATIONAL
ENDOWMENT
FOR THE ARTS

State of the Arts

NYSCA

for Dinah, again

CONTENTS

RANCHO NOTORIOUS

A Diver for the NYPD Talks to His Girlfriend

—⁓—

I can't even see my hands in front of my face
through that darkness — mud, raw sewage,
black clouds of who knows what,
gas and oil leaking out of cars
that have been shoved into the river.
But my hands have learned to see,
sliding sideways down wrinkled concrete,
over slime-coated rocks, broken glass, plastic bags,
barbed wire, as if there were a tiny eye
at the end of each finger. There are sponges down there
shaped like puffed-up lips, with silky tentacles
that retract at my touch. For some reason, grocery carts
are making their way to the river bottom.
Did I tell you about the body wrapped in plastic
and chains, and a pile of pistols, rifles,
enough to start a gun shop? Once, looking for a missing
Piper Cub, we found it next to a trainer
from World War II, both parked side by side
as if waiting for permission to take off.
People throw strange things into the river,
I don't know, some kind of voodoo — jars
filled with pig eyes, chickens with their throats slit
stuffed into burlap sacks. Everything — TVs, couches,
lamps, phone books — is down there; if we ever grow gills
and live underwater we'll have whatever we need.
Today it was a fishing boat missing for five days,
easy to find now by a certain odor seeping
through our wet suits that we call corpse soup.

Fishermen were sitting in the cabin, bloated hands
drifting as if they were swapping stories.
We tied them together and rose toward the surface
in a slow spiral. Once, I was feeling around in darkness
for this drowned lady; I was about to go back,
to call it a day, when her arms shot up
and grabbed me tight, tight around my waist.
Even when we're out of the river there's more water.
Bath, shower, bath, shower, disinfectant, rinse —
but I never feel clean. Everything seems dirty: the crowd
in the marketplace, car horns, alarms, the barking of dogs.

The Palazzo

Nobody came to the concert at the palazzo —
Which was good, since the string quartet failed to show.

Later that night, a naked woman entered the palazzo.
She laid her head on her arms and tried to sleep.
But it was so quiet there, her thoughts kept her awake.

Finally, toward dawn, she slept and was visited
By distant, wealthy relatives from America
Who wanted to buy the palazzo and its famous gardens.

The palazzo had been built three centuries before by a count
Who had three misfortunes: he was a dwarf, a hunchback,
And married to the most beautiful woman in the world.

One day she ran off with his brother,
A handsome fellow, known for his rakish ways.
Enraged, the count murdered them both
And built the palazzo to enshrine their inner organs.

He ordered an elaborate garden built around the palazzo,
A garden in which each tree and bush
Was deliberately twisted into hideous shapes.

Vines spiraled around the columns of the palazzo,
And there was a fountain of a grinning satyr
Squeezing a voluptuous woman from behind
While water spouted out of her mouth.

When the relatives flashed their checkbooks,
Wings filled the sky and carried off the palazzo to America.
In America the palazzo was small, just a gazebo.

The relatives felt cheated. Even their neighbors,
Who had never been anywhere, had bigger, better palazzos.

Star Chamber

After adventures and misadventures
we came to a kind of temple, Greek or Roman,
where it seemed pain was exalted into fine art.
What else to think about that naked man
who greeted us silently? More than naked, flayed.
The temple was set on an enormous plane
incised with a grid of interlocking lines.
Numbers were stamped on the flayed man's muscles,
which made me wonder — what if, my love,
I had to eat your flesh to survive?
I numbered you in my mind: one, the cheeks
of your face; two, your throat. But let's
not talk about that. Remember how he raised
his arm as if a grand event was about to begin?
We heard water flowing through a pool
and the strumming of light that seemed
tied to each pillar with strings, watched
shadows of pillars advance with mute intention.
Let elders in neocolonial mourning garb pass judgment
on our nightmares. Let ballerinas swing on trapezes
balancing swords on their chins and shapely women
in tights that exalt their nakedness twirl from ropes.
We've been to a circus of statues and ghosts,
peered into a chamber where constellations
were painted on the ceiling to ease painful inquisition.
In the center of this chamber, on a pedestal, a basin
that held a lover's heart. Not your curved, cello-like loveliness
seen from behind as you lay on your side, but a beating,

steaming heart. Carnal, I would call it. My Sweetmeat,
could I have trusted you if I slept? Would your breath
piercing my ear have caused blue sky to blacken
with wings? The temple was just a tiny, insignificant detail
of the galaxy. The chamber was a small version of the temple.
It was supposed to be our world. But with eyes closed
we could hear that it was a long time ago. Whirling bike tires
of a paperboy over wet pavement: a bandage ripped from skin.
Clicking of a milkman's basket: instruments, sharp, sterilized,
laid out carefully on a tray.

Wasted Lives

I am in bed trying to lull myself to sleep
imagining various methods of murdering
my neighbor's dogs. Asleep at last, I enter
a tearoom in the nineteenth century,
appropriately dressed in a greatcoat
and beaver hat, and find myself attracted
to a young woman. Her name is Thalia.
She has auburn hair, braided and coiled,
and I imagine that undone, it must reach
almost to her knees. I have a rival
for her affection, my friend Raphael,
a dandy who dresses like an artist,
loose white shirt, ascot and beret.
The three of us sit together often,
and she delights in our efforts
to keep her amused. After what seems
like a month of afternoon teas,
Raphael and I learn that she has married
a baker who joined us once — a rather
course and unattractive fellow,
we thought at the time. But she continues
to take tea with us, looking up demurely
from her cup at Raphael. One day,
sitting in the tearoom by myself,
I have to take a leak, so I rise
and make my way through the crowded,
noisy room. A man calls out to me,
and everyone is silent. "I loved that story

of yours that appeared in the *Journal*,
'Wasted Lives,' especially its ending, a young man
lying on the madam's bed in a brothel, sobbing."
Thalia, who hasn't noticed me in months,
looks up at me with renewed interest.
But I don't stop to speak to her
because I really have to pee,
and my neighbor's dogs are barking again.
Back in bed, I close my eyes and return
to the tearoom. Not much has changed.
Thalia has not been seen for a long time.
Some people think she emigrated to America
with her family. "I wonder," says Raphael,
"if she ever thinks of us?" At least, neither of us
has aged much overnight,
which in the tearoom can be a long, long time.

To My Ex-Husband

—⁓—

I sent a letter to the draft board
informing them you never registered,
called the immigration hot line,
mentioned that your so-called
secretary from Australia bought
her green card in an alley, identified
you as a fugitive in an anonymous
phone call to *America's Most Wanted*,
wrote your name on a scrap, rolled
it into a ball, sent it through a shredder,
retrieved it, jumbled up the pieces
and sat in a dark room chewing them
slowly as I invoked unspeakable names
of bat-winged demons and visualized
your profile on the post office wall,
weak chin, forehead's Neanderthal slope —
a.k.a. Mr. Sensitive, the poet who turned
a gift for metaphor toward mail fraud.
I filed your hard drive in the trash bin
right after I notified all sixty thousand
customers of your New Age Spiritual
Catalog that the packet of earth
they purchased from holy ground
in Jerusalem blessed by a famous priest
came from a backyard in El Segundo
blessed by Scotty, our bulldog.
The wrinkle cream so popular among
the ladies of Newport Beach is actually

Preparation H, and the Destroy Enemies
Juju Powder works really well for jock itch.
Ex-husband, may X be thy former name
forever deleted from the Book of Life.
May your balls be BBs as you slide back
and forth between the bony, thin thighs
of your bubble-brained bride like sandpaper
against a marble statue. May Polyhymnia,
muse of sacred poetry, who once graced
your mornings, be just another ex-lover
who says she never, never knew you.

Nobody Here but Us

In my carnival days, I used to hypnotize chickens.
I'd hold one up close and stare straight into its eyes,
and that chicken would freeze and plop over, stiff
as an old boot. Waving my arms, mumbo jumbo,
that was just showmanship. Who would pay to see
a man staring at a chicken? But they are obstinate.
That's their whole problem. Chickens are obstinate
just like apes who could talk if they wanted to.
If they wanted to, chickens could fly. I don't mean
jump from a barn or into a tree but fly, fill the sky,
migrate, rise with the spiraling vultures. You could
put one in a wind tunnel, maybe just a big, plastic
tube with a fan at one end and a couple of small
holes drilled on top, pull up and down on strings
attached to its wings, and play some stirring music
like John Philip Sousa or the theme from *Rocky*,
and that ornery chicken would still refuse to fly.
Movies, memories, dreams, they're all mixed up.
Why do I have a faded photo of three women,
heads bowed, descending a platform at a county fair,
each wearing a quilted tea cozy on her head
shaped like a chicken? Was one of them my lover?
Were they the losers in a chicken-clucking contest?
Did I really catch Richard Nixon crouching like a fox
in the red glow of my hen house? And did he say,
"Excuse me, but I thought this was a voting booth?"
Was there a gunfight? Was I carried out of town
hanging from a rail, tar and feathers my only clothing?

I seem to remember throwing a stewed chicken,
it sticking to the ceiling, plate and all, my wife crying.
They used to love my act. I'd look down from the back
of a truck at blank-faced, crossed-eyed, beak-nosed
farmers, a drum would roll, I'd put that chicken's head
into my mouth and bite it off. The crowd would scream.
I'd spit the head into some lady's lap — flap my elbows,
knock my knees together, strut, cluck, cock-a-doodle-do
and spin that chicken over my head, spraying blood like rain.

Just Like Saint Peter

Chickenhead makes me think of Jesus. Even though Jesus died on the cross for our sins and Chickenhead was just a hood who died hanging from a meat hook. First, take the Romans — Italian, right? In other words, gangsters. Take hanging from a cross and hanging from a meat hook. Both ways, you die slow.

Chickenhead used to shoot the heads off chickens in his backyard when he was a kid. Jesus used to play with birds when he was a kid too. Except instead of blowing them apart he would put them together.

Chickenhead was a big shot on the block. In more ways than one, since he weighed three hundred pounds. When Chickenhead got in the back of his Cadillac it would tilt to one side. Jesus was big in his neighborhood too. But he was skinny. When Jesus would get on a donkey — maybe it was an old, decrepit, almost dead donkey — that donkey would trot along skimming over stones as if it had wings.

Jesus made people mad. Chickenhead made people mad. Skimming a little off the top's OK, it's expected. But after Chickenhead bought that second Cadillac, and after what he did to that Gypsy girl in the back room of the cleaners with her dad forced to watch, he had to go.

The Romans had dice. We had dice. The Romans had a wooden cross. We had a meat hook. The Romans had spears and vinegar. We had a bucket of cold water and one of those electric cattle pokers.

Chickenhead hung there. We'd give him a splash and an electric goose once in a while. His whole body would shimmer, all blubbery. Took Jesus three hours. Took Chickenhead three days.

Jesus got famous. First guy to beat Death at his own game. Nobody remembers Chickenhead but me. And if some stranger, a cop maybe, asked, Did I know Chickenhead? I'd play it safe just like Saint Peter when he heard that cock crow once, twice, three times: I'd say, I never knew nobody named Chickenhead.

The Golden Ones

A support group of prospectors' wives disappeared in Brazil. The prospectors, suspecting an Indian raid or terrorist abduction, hired a detective to find their missing wives.

The detective made discreet inquiries at the Hotel Oro Verde, where the wives were last seen in a suite on the twentieth floor. According to the night clerk, sounds of a riotous party were heard issuing from their rooms just prior to their disappearance.

A boy, who stood outside the hotel charging tourists a dollar each to pose for a photo with his pet iguana, reported a cascade of straw hats that fell or were thrown from a balcony during the party. The iguana on his shoulder was fascinated by the boy's fluttering, mime-like gestures, as he described how silently and slowly those hats drifted toward the cobblestones. The detective took this all down when he interviewed the boy. He also added that the iguana's face made him think of Buster Keaton.

The detective followed the trail of the missing wives up the Amazon and deep into the interior. When questioned directly about the missing wives, the natives feigned ignorance. But at night, sitting around their fires, they told stories about a group of fantastically beautiful women they called Las Doradas. Las Doradas: how wildly they danced and beat their drums, how they sang and smeared their naked bodies with yellow mud containing flecks of gold.

Confessions of an Exhibitionist

Watching you watch yourself,
as you undress slowly before a mirror
in sandalwood-scented candlelight,
I confess that I too am an exhibitionist,
although I never show myself in public,
and I never show myself in private.
After all, didn't the universe retract,
as if in shame, space retreating
from nothingness at the very moment
of its creation like a coquettish bride
hiding from her beloved? That is why
I only reveal myself to you, and then only
in complete darkness. I avoid cameras,
claiming I'm enrolled in the secret witness
protection program. To discourage myself
from seducing or being seduced, I wear silk
bikini-style briefs that are torn to shreds.
I remember my first day of school, the classroom
completely silent except for the click-click
of the metal taps on my new shoes against linoleum
like the sound of two crawfish scurrying
across an abandoned train station.
I knew all eyes were turned toward me.
But I sat there with my eyes closed,
feeling safe and alone at the still center
of attention, as if the classroom
had turned itself inside out and left me
quite content to be stranded on the other side.

Some people, you for instance, might enjoy
writhing under a blue spotlight on a tabletop
to Tom Jones's version of "You Can Leave Your Hat On"
in a smoky haze of a roomful of mercenaries
and Asian businessmen. Whereas I would prefer
to hide myself by revealing myself. I like to imagine
peeling off my clothing, then my skin, my flesh,
plucking out my heart, my most intimate inner organs,
and finally, unsnapping my bones one by one
until nothing is left but my skeletal hands, outstretched,
open in the universal gesture of nothing to hide.

A Death in Larkspur Canyon

Going out that evening with the garbage
I saw something crouched below me.
Then it rose — an owl — dark, silent,
billowing like a scarf thrown in the air.
Just another sparrow taken up, taken apart.
I left what little remained, feathers and beak,
there on the front stairs, out of sight of anyone
who might pass by on the footpath below the picket fence.

Muriel, our neighbor, died that night. A widow —
almost friendless except for Mrs. Dodge, who was one hundred
years old. Sometimes you'd see her driving Muriel into town
in a vintage Studebaker, head barely clearing the top
of the steering wheel, zigzagging down the narrow canyon road,
Muriel with one hand on the dashboard, the other on her hat,
who scattered seed for birds on the front porch,
popcorn for deer in the backyard,
who stood outside each morning pretending
to be waiting for someone while she stuffed peanuts
in the cracks of a redwood tree for the squirrels.
Muriel who could be heard shouting at her dogs and cats
when they ate out of the wrong bowls, Muriel who died
because she would not go to the hospital
and leave her animals alone over the weekend.

Monday morning, Muriel's sister and brother-in-law arrived
and shook their heads at the house full of old newspapers,
dog hair, and cat piss. They were followed by a clean-up crew —

carpenters banging, whining saws, and slaphappy painters
blasting their radios, until one day there was silence —
and a young woman in a page-boy haircut pulled up in a BMW,
stepped out, and stumbled to one knee as she planted
a For-Sale sign like an explorer claiming new territory.

I am still wondering about what I found on the stairs
a few nights after I saw that owl. Something had carried
from a distance and placed, so carefully on the gray pile
of feathers, six red berries from a pyracantha bush.

The Laws of Salvage

Returning to Macuto, we may follow the driver
as he leaps out of a bus, yelling that it's about
to burst into flames, may endure the homicidal
pounding of a *peñero* smashed through waves
by a teenager. We may even stroll out on a coral reef
until we lose sight of land and stand in the ocean —
three hundred sixty degrees — just us, the sea
and a circling barracuda that's planning to intercept
any bright fish I may hook and is not impressed
by my attempts to poke him away with my fly rod.
You will stare into the pocket of each wave
looking for loose change while I wait
for tiny triangular mirrors to flash their messages.

At the Macuto airport, taxiing airplanes will avoid the goats,
and the baggage cart shall be a wheelbarrow pushed
and pulled by arguing children. Between flights
they'll give each other rides and haul around the small
black-and-white dog that chases the planes as they glide in.
Even El Presidente himself will greet us as if
he has known us for years, has read our poems,
and can, perhaps due to an elegiac wisdom of high office,
see into our souls. He will pass before us flanked
by beribboned dignitaries and slit-eyed soldiers
carrying Uzis, glance at us standing to the rear
of a crowd and nod, saying, "Bueno," meaning, I approve,
you have chosen well to find your way back to Macuto.

It was at Macuto that we endured a solitude inhabited
by black lizards, black squirrels, and one
oil-soaked albatross that had come here to die.
It was at Macuto that I gradually became ragged
and dissolute, hanging around the airport,
leaning on a cyclone fence, sneering at rich fishermen
and aging Nazis who arrived to catch a yacht
that would take them to a private, unnamed island.
That's me in a Panama hat and remains of what was
an expensive silk shirt I found on the beach
after a wild night at La Casa de Rosa, the night
house painters whitewashed the chief of police
while he lay passed out in the cabana.

If we return to Macuto, we'll be rewarded by a precision
of piratical frigate birds and the crazy splashing of pelicans
crashing into surf like suitcases falling from the sky.
At Rosa's, we'll cling to the very same bed we drove
into town and had trouble parking, the bed
that tilts from side to side while bobbing into an inlet
where red parrots decorate black mangrove branches.
We'll listen for a distant artillery of heat lightning
and sometimes see the green slash at sunset that cleaves
the horizon like a saber, fusing its imperfect luminescence.
We'll walk the beach at midnight, lean against an overturned
rowboat with our heads tilted back over the keel. You'll see,
it's just like I told you, all upside-down constellations

in this part of the world are salvage, and we'll claim them for ourselves, ignoring the fine legal distinctions between what has been jettisoned and what has fallen away.

Men Without Women

—∿—

Returning from the airport through pouring rain,
he found a newsletter from the synagogue
and his eyes landed right on the ad
for a memorial plot — he couldn't help it,
he thought of his wife's plane.
Shaking his head he went upstairs, took off
his shoes, lay down and felt a hand squeeze
his foot; a gentle yet firm pressure on his arch.
Had his wife's spirit risen from some steaming,
snowy cornfield and flown back to touch him?
No, he said to himself, shaking his head again,
this time he would not stumble step by step
down an evolutionary stairway. No mounds
of gnawed rib bones from Leon's in the sink.
No leftover static from the Big Bang flickering
on his blue, icy skin at 3 AM. Not his wife's
favorite Depression-ware salad bowl flung from
the porch in a misguided effort at shaking
it dry, nor the curvature in her French grapefruit knife
straightened out, not even fragments of the heavy,
shin-rapping glass coffee table stuffed in a trash can
and covered with newspapers like a murder victim.
He went up to his office, turned on his computer —
that's when he heard the banging, and with each bang,
he blinked. Or were the lights switching on and off?
He ran downstairs, outside into the alley
and saw the house light up in a flash as electricity
popped and sizzled, arching from a broken glass gauge

into the rain and tree branches. He smelled burnt wire.
Dashing under a spray of sparks, he hit the main switch,
then went inside and called the power company.
No power, no heat. He put on a bulky sweater,
his Gortex hat and after-ski boots. He sat waiting
for the repair men. It was getting dark and the rain
beat against the house. Maybe he would sit there for days.
Maybe his wife would return and find him still there
wrapped in a blanket. Enough of that. Repair men would come.
Then he could watch the news for reports of any plane crashes.

Vernon

Vernon of brick smokestacks, of circuitous
slaughter houses, of meat packing, of heavy
and light industry, of wrong exit.
Vernon, where I found myself not
on the way to the airport.
Vernon, where the ribbon of concrete
that resembled the freeway entrance
was just the skeleton of a Roman aqueduct.
Vernon, where I slammed on my brakes,
effectively trapping the only pedestrian
in Vernon against a bridge railing.
"Do you know the way to the airport?" I said.
"Do you know the way to the airport?" he said,
apparently frightened into echolalia.
"No, but I do know the acrid smell of fear,"
I replied, as I sped off while watching him
mouth my words in the rearview mirror.
I thought of the murdered convict stuffed
into a fifty-gallon drum and shipped via UPS
to an animal rendering plant in Vernon.
VERNON, I cried out as I sped between warehouses
and self-storage facilities, as my wife's plane
flashed Fasten Seat Belts and flight attendants
were making sure all seats were in an upright position,
trays latched back, GOD HELP ME, I'M IN VERNON.
Vernon, a painting by de Chirico: a solitary tower,
an archway, shadows leaning against pylons,
a plaster face reflecting sunlight from the bottom

of a well representing an abyss of despair.
Vernon, where I prayed my wife's plane would be late,
that she would step carefully from the hatch
through the rubbery mouth of a landing dock,
prepared to apologize for my long wait
and never know that I too had come vast distances
and emerged through a tunnel, had been face to face
with Vernon, my own private Vernon,
Vernon of no entrance, no exit, closed ramp,
under construction, detour, go back, severe tire damage.

His Wife, Folded

A man folded his wife into three sections, put them in his pocket and went walking by the sea. He touched her with his hand, which he kept in his pocket.

Occasionally he would take her out and hold her to his face, as if he were studying a picture from his wallet. Was the man cruel? No, he had often heard her say that she wanted to be something small that he carried in his pocket.

The wife thought that being folded into three sections was like having sisters, like looking at herself in a mirror with three panels — true mirrors, not false ones that turn everything backward.

As the sun was setting, the man took his wife out of his pocket. He built a little mound of sand. He scooped out a moat around it and placed her on top like three cards on a table.

Sitting on the beach this way, his wife remembered her childhood by the lake: wet sand in her fist, cold then warm; her tin bucket, blue with big white stars; her yellow shovel, its serious heft when she pried at the sand. A playfulness of foam touched her ankles like the lacy hem of a gigantic skirt. She could sit there forever.

Aware that she was in a private reverie, the man walked farther down the beach. He brought her here often, although he disliked the ocean. It was, as he once said to his wife, "too big." Perhaps next time he would place her in an envelope . . . address it to himself. She would like that.

What Passes for Sleep

Sometimes foghorns and sirens stain the night,
and a stale imprint of the moon against my window
resembles a bruise. Sometimes it is so quiet I hear
the swishing of my blood as I shift, carefully, not to wake you.
I get that floating sensation: as if my hands, arms, legs, torso,
were all absorbed into my big, big head. Air clenches tight
against my skin, and I am bobbing, swaying to my pulse.
Often I'm convinced by vibration and a smoldering crucible
of dark cloud on the horizon that I'm on an airplane.
The captain is speaking through a hole in his larynx and may,
as we slip between mountain ledges, start to bark.
Not one of your high yip-yips or deep woofs, but a raspy
burnishing of aluminum that passes for sleep
in this neighborhood. But then again, I may be just one
of a cast of itinerant players whose van is coasting
down an incline into memory. The driver may be asleep,
which is just as well — he's a dangerous man, former
paratrooper who carries a bowie knife in his boot.
I am in the back seat smooching with my lover.
She's a look-alike for Anita Ekberg, a fact destined
to get us all in trouble as we head south and cross
the last checkpoint. Sometimes I think I am a bullfighter.
I waltz cows around the rings of border towns where
I'm known as Jaime Bravo. You'll find my real name
in the *Encyclopedia of Bullfighting*, my picture
(page 223) taken that day, many years ago, in Barcelona
when they gave me two ears and a tail. I lied.
I am not a bullfighter. I am a passenger on a train,

cooling my forehead against a window.
I have confused shirts waving from clotheslines
with the pages of a book I have been reading,
a story that begins slowly, then picks up speed
as the night turns its back on me.

Intimations of Ratoon

—〜〜—

Early film industry jargon
describing the first primitive
attempts at animation.
A triumphant cry
bursting from a crowd
at the circus suddenly cut
short by a gasp of horror.
An overwhelming desire
to spit tobacco juice
on marble floors.
A pain in your heart
when you remember
the call you did not return
from a friend later killed
during artillery practice.
When you wake in a park
by a lake, with a prickling
sensation that your blood
is seeping into the water.
Passersby will know you're deep
in ratoon by the way the book
of poems you should have written
slides down your chest.
When you close your eyes
and see a hypnogogic image
of yourself amorously
pursuing the rear end
of a departing Volkswagen.

The suspicion that some
small thing you did not do
has sealed your fate.
A typhoon that sideswipes
a pier, depositing many
rodents. Tendrils of desire
blossoming unexpectedly.
A military drumbeat
that signifies surrender —
rat-a-tat-tat of snare drums
followed by a deep boom-boom.

Against Frog

You pop-eyed
bandy-legged
scum-slurper,
squatting on
a lily-pad
all night
filling air
with that
burp voice,
how long
will you
insult the moon?
Some prince —
you eat
your children.
I've seen
your mama's head
peering out
of your throat,
seen you
on PBS humped
around your lady's
back, your muscular
legs all shining
in a frothy
gelatin of eggs
while some actor
whose career

is sliding drones
on hypnotically
as you repeat
repeat your one
your only
two-stroke song.
Someday you'll
squeal, reaching
that high note
at last, so beautiful —
Frog Hits High C!
Bravo! Bellisimo!
as Mr. Water Snake
clamps on to
your webbed toes
and pulls.

The Ceremony

The poetry workshop graduated from robbing filling stations to liquor stores, and their notoriety became the talk of the circuit. Not since the days of Black Bart had poet-thieves attracted such attention.

But Martin, a young poet in the workshop, became despondent after reading a biography of Clyde Barrow and Bonnie Parker. Apparently Bonnie was a poet, too, and Martin could not get the refrain from her last poem out of his head, "And it's death for Bonnie and Clyde."

Nick, the leader of the workshop, had been saving a tidbit for just this occasion. "Did you know," he said to his young protégé, "that Gypsies always name their dancing bears Martin?"

This made Martin smile. However, during their next robbery, he became enraged and bludgeoned a slow-moving cashier with a crucifix he had been attempting to pass off as a gun hidden in a pocket of his overcoat. The clerk lay writhing on the floor. Martin, distraught, covered his face in dismay. Nick noticed that what the clerk had been concealing under his foot was not an alarm button but half of a map. It was a crude drawing of a mountain range. In what signified a hidden valley was the cryptic word "Chuck-a-Luck."

Nick came to attention. He recognized it from a movie, *Rancho Notorious*. In the movie, "Chuck-a-Luck" was a roulette game, but it was also the name of a secret ranch where bandits would find refuge and happiness. Even though in the distance he could hear sirens, he stood there smiling, convinced that somehow he was about to make his way home.

But first — providing they made it back to their hideout — he would have to do something to distract Martin. He would tell him about the ceremony — yes, the ceremony Gypsies perform to cure sadness: how the sad person lies on the floor, shirtless, and allows a bear to place its foot on his chest, while all the Gypsies, standing in a circle, chant in Romany, *Ajde, ajde, malo Martine, ajde*: "Dance, dance, little Martin, dance."

The Detective and the Curio

One afternoon, while wandering through an arcade,
melancholy drove me to purchase a plaster buffalo.
Why should I want it? It wasn't even well made.

Looking down at it, I stood so stiff
the petals of a night-blooming flower could have opened
        in my shadow.
I had that sinking feeling, like a balloonist

drifting over the sea,
suspended in the sights of an assassin with a crossbow —
or as if I had just tripped over a severed hand that clutched
        a note addressed to me.

Later, I sat at a bar with my prize on the counter
        ignoring insinuations of the barmaid
concerning my pink — did I tell you it was pink? — plaster
        buffalo.
Was I on a treasure hunt, or was it some kind of crusade

to save indigenous art of the carnival,
she wanted to know. I ignored her, the matchbook covers,
        jokes on napkins. All that imploding status quo
was just so much reflection of ice cubes on the wall

as far as I cared. I'd had enough
of this lady, although I did give some thought

to the two of us in a seaside bungalow
while I fingered the key to my handcuffs.

I could see us lying side by side beneath a window,
        her skin all rosy in the glow
of sunset reflected off the underside of bumpy clouds,
and on the windowsill, a pink plaster buffalo.

Shark

I am the best, I never lose at tennis.
My eyes, like buttons, blank, opaque and dead,
make nervous adversaries tremble and miss.
No beads of sweat dot my bullet-shaped head.
I am far away, not that I'm haughty — no,
I'm really thinking of the three groupies
I'll take back to my motel room. I'll show
them in and eat everything — pleated skirts, panties
with the cute printing across the derrière:
Hot Stuff! U.S.D.A. Prime Cut! Watch It!
Sometimes I wonder what it's like to despair,
to lose, to be the other, the weak opponent.
How boring, my life: I'm never caught off guard,
I never stop, never sleep, never swim backward.

Loan Shark

It was the last quarter of the moon's surrender.
Laura said, "You've got ice water for blood
and a hunk of rock for a heart." "True," I told her,
as I straightened my tie, and night, like a flood
filled the window with darkness that was my mirror.
What was left of the moon was caught
in the naked, white branches of a tree, so bare
I thought of a drowned man illumined by a searchlight.
Laura slid up behind me, in her black slip
all alabaster arms and pearl necklace. "We're ghosts,"
she said, "so transparent we hardly exist,
two shimmering puffs of gossamer dust."
Meanwhile clouds circled the moon like sharks
cruising, turning away, turning back, like sharks.

Elite Syncopations

—⁓—

Glancing at the wicker night stand I had just brought
for her, my mother, for a moment, stepped back in time.
Wasn't this the same night stand she had in her room
in Mexico when she was a child more than sixty years ago?

And when I happened to play Scott Joplin's
"Elite Syncopations" on the phonograph, she smiled;
back in Mexico she was a child again on her way to school —
she had been told to hurry past the cantinas —
but she and her girlfriends loved to dance to the music
that rippled from behind swinging doors,
music that sparkled with a touch of sadness.

Once she told me how she ran with her mother
across a courtyard while bullets pinged and spattered.
"Lie low," her mother had whispered, as they pressed
their faces into dust and her mother threw her black rebozo
over her head. . . . Now I am remembering a bus trip
we never took, deep into the interior. Second class,

nights of no sleep, our sweat odorless, as if we took baths
from the inside out. It's a battle of raised and slammed
windows, of lose your seat if you get up to pee, wooden
slats pressed into our bones, and ignore that man
masturbating under his jacket. The three nice nuns
who sit behind us have something to show us,

a fetus one of them keeps in a small jar of formaldehyde.
"Viejito" they call him, wise old man with wrinkled brow,
little blue man sleeping. The hills loom up darker than night
and my mother says we are passing her hometown.
"What's it called?" I ask. "It has no name," she says,
"and the people there are bad, gangsters, all of them."

The little man who knows everything seems to agree,
as he floats, tilting this way and that, lying low, always level
to the earth. Never having been born, he believes everything.
Yes, he seems to say to himself, with just a hint of a smile,
gangsters, all of them, the little table, the music quick and slow,
your mother skipping along on her way to school.

Paducah

How'd this classy dame get on top of my Jaguar?
How'd I get a Jaguar?

Miss Night, Noche, Lila Tov, whatever
you claim your name is. Dirty blonde bangs,
black evening gown, strapless —

you drip off the hood,
slide expensive-smelling, small cleavage past my face —

I expect to hear "In the Mood" but you're smarter than that,
smarter than "Twilight Time" by the Harmonicats.

It's "Paducah," not a town in Kentucky
but "Paducah" by the Chocolate Dandies;

trombones, clarinets, sax,
Lonnie Johnson on guitar my all-time-ten-cents-a-dance-
I-want-to-be-where-you-are-put-me-in-a-trance song.

It's 1928. We're slow dancing,
revolving in a net of tiny mirrors,
just drunk enough to know it doesn't get any better,

even if it's almost time to see
that I'm embracing air —

to sit up startled in bed, missing you, all sweaty
from this what-have-I-done-with-my-life scenario.
But listen, while I fumble with the keys:

right now: the song slows, stops,
someone rings a little bell, heavenly,
like an elevator door opening —
and it's "Paducah," "Paducah" once again.

Odds Against Tomorrow

—⁓—

A man always dreams about what he wants or what
he's afraid of. I was really wailing on my sax
at the Blackhawk — the music dangling, twirling
slowly in a spiral like a mobile made of black
and white rectangles when the cash register chimed in
right on key with my solo, and everything
went silent: reflections off glasses, the blue light
over the mirror, red glow of cigarettes — everything
became a dim flickering of crab claws in silty water.
Once I jumped off a window ledge,
after a lifetime, it seemed, of searching for this girl.
Not my type really. Thin, the kind of girl, if you didn't like,
you'd call mousy. No tits. Tomboy, too. Anyway,
I gave up looking for her, and just as I was leaning
into tomorrow too far to go back, I saw a door open,
she walked in and I knew she was looking for me.
I woke with this sadness in my stomach, something
without a cure, a crazy longing to get back in the past
and stay there. I wondered, if I threw myself out a window,
would I see her again? Sometimes I pace my room, smoking,
the lights off, thinking of maybe calling my ex-wife, Kitty.
She always said I'd end up in a room like this: bathroom
down the hall, hot plate, a sink I piss in. I'm pacing, smoking,
listening over and over to Monk's "Misterioso." The notes
slightly off balance, hesitant, excited, like a man climbing up
and down a ladder in the dark. I pace around my room step
by step until I hear the silver slash of Art Blakey's drumroll —
that's my cue to stop, turn, and pace again in the opposite direction.

Birdlike Sonata

There was music in the rain
as it beat on the tin roof, birdlike.
It was then they finally did dance
together, there in the kitchen
of Tiki Bob's, under a tropical plant,
and the song they'd sing

about it they'd never sing.
They were lost in that rain,
under a blossoming plant
that hovered over them, birdlike
with wings extended across the kitchen
observing their odd dance

their awkward, monsoon dance.
He never heard her sing,
but they did shuffle across that kitchen
while he deciphered the word that the rain
rang metallic across the roof, the birdlike,
Malaysian, *rimchin, rimchim*. He tried to plant

his footsteps in hers, to plant
a seed in each step of their swing dance.
Into the empty ballroom, birdlike,
in caution, they slid to imagined music: "Sing,
Sing, Sing," tom-toms pounding like rain,
busboys staring at them from the kitchen,

waitress and bartender smiling in the kitchen.
Was there a moment to plant
a thought, suggest the butterfly step, rain
causing their arms to slither, intertwine, dance
all on their own? *Not to be* the tin roof did sing
as he saw how birdlike

she slipped away, carefully, how birdlike.
Now a busboy strums his ukulele in the kitchen;
the bartender's wet finger makes glasses sing
Yes for dancers without music under the plant,
dancing their two-martini afternoon dance —
it was really quite warm and steamy in that rain,

and she was birdlike, they say, a wavering plant.
Suddenly tropical, the kitchen, they began to dance,
though it never happened, we sing them and the rain.

Those Moments

Like the night in Jerusalem when,
after having dinner in what had once been
a crusader castle, I returned to my circular room
in the tower and, as I peered through a slit
built for archers with long bows (convenient
for pouring burning oil on infidels scaling walls
with scimitars clenched between their teeth),
saw dawn paint hills and misty orchards
the powdery pastels of a tourist painting, quite lovely,
except it seemed to me that I had just left the dinner table.

Even stars can be confusing, like that night
on a freighter crossing the Mediterranean Hava
began kissing her way up through the hair
on my arms and stars would not stay put —
one pulsing like a flare, another taking off, swirling
across an entire sky like the pointer of a distracted lecturer
in a planetarium, and maybe it was that sudden giant

of black thundercloud who appeared in a clear sky
and tripped over a mountain that made me stumble
through an aspen grove unable to stop following myself.
Those moments when I'm driving and forget
where I'm going, when I feel as if I were not moving
at all, as if I were in a movie of someone driving.
A moment when I'm not quite sure if I'm looking
at a pulsing sea anemone or the ebb and flow
of a symphony orchestra tuning up, or maybe

I'm just pleasantly surprised when I open my eyes
to see a green wave suspended in the pinnacle
when the ocean becomes completely silent,
and you lying beside me — when even the word *us*,
unmoored from its meaning, could roll and float away,
caught up in turning of houses, piers,
and crumbling crenelations of the ancient hillsides.

Rancho Notorious

—◦◦◦—

Ray stands on a hillside overlooking his hometown.
It's almost dawn, and as he watches the streetlights
go out, he tries to remember something, anything:
like the name of Red Ryder's little Indian sidekick,
or who played drums on "Big Noise from Winnetka."
He remembers forgetting his own name when he was
shaken out of sleep by a grinning policeman. Maybe
he should call Lita. She'll remember him.
He's not angry at her for hiding behind a door,
clutching a kitchen knife the last time he came to see her.
Does she still drive race cars and dress up
as a dance hall girl, just like Marlene Dietrich
in *Rancho Notorious*? If she asks him where he's been,
he'll say he doesn't remember. If she asks him
to wear a black silk cowboy shirt and answer
to the name Frenchie, he won't refuse. He descends
the hillside, thinking of her, Lita — Lita placing her foot
on a chair, flipping her can-can skirt over her thigh
as she tucks a derringer beneath her garter belt.
Lita — will she throw her head back and laugh,
showing off her luscious throat, her felt choker
with its little diamond stud? Now he remembers
the drummer's name on "Big Noise from Winnetka."
Of course, it was Ray, just like his. Maybe it *was* him.
As he dials he imagines numbers spinning skyward
in a game of vertical roulette, like sparks —
as if a burly orderly struck two electrodes together.
It's almost dawn but the sky seems to darken

for just a moment and he feels a chill, feels suddenly
wary, like a reporter who has finagled his way
into a mysterious hospital; a rider descending a trail
whose horse stops, refusing to go forward; as if he were
strolling along a crowed street, whistling, and had just
noticed he is being followed by a long, black limousine.

La Loteria

I'm the flimflam man, El Bailarin,
a mantra of dissolving possibilities.
The syntax of night plays havoc with sleep.
You are the reason I dance bolero.

A mantra of dissolving possibilities
is the bouquet I offer.
You are the reason I dance bolero.
All the polls are in agreement.

Is the bouquet I offer
dangerous in moonlight?
All the polls are in agreement,
our shadows have already eloped.

Dangerous in moonlight,
that's how I'd describe your skin.
Our shadows have already eloped.
See the ladder leaning against the sky —

that's how I'd describe your skin,
an emblem of vanishing.
See the ladder leaning against the sky.
See the moon painted by a child —

an emblem of vanishing.
The syntax of night plays havoc with sleep.
See the moon painted by a child.
I'm the flimflam man, El Bailarin.

Certain Images, Excluded from My Poems,
Form a Parade

—⁓—

When an iceberg pulled by a team of white horses comes sliding
down the boulevard, the crowd, which had been so festive —
whistling, hooting, throwing hats in the air — grows silent.

Almost silent are ten Kikuyu warriors striding in slow motion,
one clenched fist shooting up every ten paces as they expel
a loud hiss in unison, making a sizzling sound, like the shallow
rush of sea that slides onto a beach between waves.

Faint at first then louder is the one-two, one-two-three
clack of the milkmaids, each tapping a wooden ladle against
a wooden pail, faces flushed, braids stiff with desert dust,
blue eyes fixed on the horizon, as if they could see
a snow-covered peak taking shape in distant haze.

Here comes the fossilized remains of a regiment
of Assyrian infantry that disappeared
in a sandstorm three thousand years ago.
Their spear tips, protruding from papier-mâché dunes,
shine like mica. Now a classical motif — the three faces
of the moon, in her guise as the Great Mother,
symbolized by a waitress, a bank teller, and a meter maid.
They fling candies wrapped in foil, silver dollars,
and parking tickets at the men in the crowd.

Who is it that comes more splendidly arrayed than the rest,
gold buckles on black velvet sashes, silver badges shining in
          the sun?

It is the poets, a contingent from the Emily Dickinson Brigade
of the Chaparral Society, quite impressive as they drop
to one knee in unison and rap against the blacktop with their batons.

Should we join the parade, take up the rear and follow? Who can
resist the young Chinese girl in a black leather miniskirt?
Pounding, slowly pounding on her bass drum, boom-boom, boom-
boom-boom — Morse code for remember, remember, do not
forget, her knees high-stepping to the rhythm. She leads us
down concrete stairs to the dance floor in the basement
of the art museum, where the band is waiting for us
among gray columns and rectangular pools of still water.

The Room

There is a man who, every night
of his life, wakes up in the same room.
He tries to read a book called *The Poetics
of Space*, which he thinks may be about
the room, but this only makes him
sleep, and when he wakes he's in
the same room. Maybe he's in Paris,
but Paris is the room. He's driving
through the room, which is now
Kansas, and every front yard
has a trampoline with one child
bouncing to see if there is a horizon.
Perhaps the room is a cell stacked
in tiers of cells and he hears cries,
laughter, catcalls cascading into
kaleidoscopic echoes and Duke,
Duke, Duke, Duke of Earl. Or he's
in the schoolyard and his friends
sit on a bench slapping their thighs,
their chests, tapping their feet, chanting,
Ham bone ham bone, where you be —
but the schoolyard resembles the room.
So he rubs his hand against the wall,
feels a flowered texture of wallpaper
underneath layers of paint, looks out
the window at the sky — pale summer gray
rolling in from the ocean. Yes, it's the same
room, a room that's as big as the world.

Legends of the West

———

Raymond Washington is in love
with Annie Oakley.
She comes to him in a vision.
Well, not exactly —
but he dreams he's at work,
sweeping through the stacks
in the library when a book
falls off the shelf,
and he hears a voice say
something like "Okra"
or "Okie" or "OK."
Sometimes, as he sweeps
his way through the library,
a book falls at his feet, open
to a picture of Annie Oakley.
There is something about her eyes —
a serious person in history,
someone he can look up to,
Lady Wing Shot, Little Missy.
Each year, on her birthday,
he paints her portrait,
frames it in crisscross patterns
like ciphers in a secret alphabet.
Each year, on her birthday,
he lights candles in her honor,
imagines himself standing
in a crowd, right below her
while she prances on parade,

on a high-stepping palomino —
with Wild Bill, Sitting Bull,
all the stars of the Wild West Show.
And if she calls to him, "Raymond,
Raymond," pulling off her buckskin-
fringed glove, can he resist —
something bright in her shining hand,
a ticket with a hole shot through it?

El Zapato

Not the wooden spoon,
primordial source
of sweetness and pain,
flying across the kitchen —
I barely bothered to duck.
Not my father undoing his belt —
I would be gone before he'd whack
the tabletop in a sample *nalgada*,
but my mother's shoe, El Zapato:
its black leather soft as the mouth
of an old, toothless dog, black laces
crisscrossing its long tongue
all the way up, heavy sole and thick
square high heel. Shoe from a special
old lady store, shoe from olden days,
puritanical shoe, *bruja* shoe, peasant
shoe, Gypsy shoe, shoe for *zapateo*
on the grave of your enemy, shoe
for dancing the twisted, bent
over dance of *los viejitos*.
Not the pain, humiliating clunk
of leather striking upside my head,
but her aim, the way I knew that even
if I ran out the kitchen door,
down the back stairs and leapt
the fence, when I glanced over my
shoulder El Zapato, prototype
of the smart bomb, would be there,

its primitive but infallible radar
honed in on my back. Not the shoe
for suicidal anger of come out of hiding
or I'll throw myself out the window.
Not the shoe for carpet-chewing
Hitler anger — the throwing herself
down, taking an edge of rug
between her teeth anger. But the shoe
for everyday justice she could unlace,
whip off and throw faster than Paladin
draws his gun, shoe that could hunt
me down like the Texas Rangers,
even if it took years, even if she died
while she was throwing her shoe,
even if she managed to throw it
from the ramparts of heaven, the way
she threw it from a third story window
while I stood half a block away, laughing
at her with my friends, thinking,
it could never hit me from this far,
until I stood suddenly alone,
abandoned by my cowardly friends,
alone in the frozen cross-eyed knowledge
that El Zapato, black, smoking with righteousness,
was slowly, inevitably spinning toward my forehead.

Star Motel, Truckee

What she likes best about the Star Motel
are the train whistles late at night.
Their undulant, moaning wails are angels,
wavering, transparent angels, made of light.

She watches them drift over the tracks
through freight yards, trailer parks,
right through houses, barely noticing
the sleepers curled up like question marks.

Couples have arrived for the New Year's party —
travel vests, Bermuda shorts, straw hats, slightly sinister,
as if they had been taught to be together,
been taught gestures, their forced, loud laughter.

She hears them making love through walls:
steady, repetitive, without cries or climax
like some sort of squeaking, apocalyptic machine —
soothing almost, like the trains over the tracks

before they pick up speed. Does their being here
have something to do with those angular shadows,
or the way mountains tilt into empty space
and seem hunched over, as if expecting a blow?

And the angels — now she sees them in daylight,
even with her eyes closed. Something's about to happen.
That's why they sit on tree branches, stand in the river;
so many angels downtown, she walks right through them.

Cat's Cradle

Notice how the man standing
at the freeway entrance, pretending
he's waiting for a carpool, strokes
a string that holds his briefcase together.
Do you remember an insistence of a kite
pulling at your wrist?

Now recall a skate key on a string
bouncing against your chest, the indecipherable
knot of fishing line that suddenly shot
through the guides and disappeared
into black water. Consider the Gordian knot:
was it a kind of book, some ancient, lunar
knowledge encoded in twine that Alexander
could not decipher? These are things
you can think about while waiting
at an intersection for the long,
long procession of a child's funeral to pass.

Follow your thoughts up to the level of clouds.
Now stay there awhile, as if
you had slipped into the cogs
of the wind's machinery, which,
if you could see them, would resemble
bright, braided coils ascending,
descending . . .

Now watch the traffic
weave and unweave. All the cars
seem part of the same procession,
all the cars blurred together are like string —
the kind you drape from your fingers
to tell a story: *There was a cat, there
was a cradle, and a man wandering
with nothing in his pockets but two candles
and a matchbox* — the kind of string you unwind
through a cave to find your way out.

But you are above all that,
like a man suspended from a hang glider
who has stepped delicately off a precipice,
cutting his ties to earth —
whose shadow, seen from a distance
by bored fishermen drifting around
and around in the smell of diesel fuel,
undulates across white cliffs
as dark, enormous wings.

Dangerous Hats

I was trying on a hat
in the Bounty Hunter Hat Shop
on East Hyman Street
in Aspen, Colorado, when I suddenly
became much taller.
I looked down at my wife
and smiled with one eyebrow raised,
like a pirate inspecting
the latest batch of hostages.

I put another hat on and I was James Dean,
leaning back in a chair on a front porch
with my foot on the railing, a snakeskin
cowboy boot sliding out of my Levi's.
Squinting into the heat lightning
that lit up the horizon, chewing on a toothpick,
I thought of you, old friend, and wondered

if I'd ever see you again, striding
toward me taking shape in the haze,
and what hat would be tilted rakishly
on your head? Not the captain's cap
from your sailing days
or the ten-gallon from Montana.
Not that creamy confection you won
from a millionaire in Nepal.
Not the black cap you stole
from a drunk SWAT cop

in a trucker's bar in West Texas.
Not the green explosion of quetzal feathers
from the Amazon you traded for a shrunken head
or the hat that survived
a machete attack in the Mexican desert.

No, if I should see you again
you'll be wearing some hat I can't imagine now.
Some boomerang that you could twirl away
over treetops, that would disappear and then return,
suddenly appearing at your feet days later.
Some hat with a fiery smell of danger,
a hat snatched off the head
of the devil himself while he lay sleeping
by his private trout stream in the underworld.

Ice

I remember footpaths worn smooth,
wooden swords in our belts,
thorns pulling at our shirts,

cardboard forts, a rope on a limb
where a hill dropped off,
houses tumbled and a sharp

edge of ocean leaned into the sky.
It was in these bushes where we hid,
three boys watching three young men

peel clothing from their girlfriends
and slice it into little strips,
which they hung from branches

like offerings to some tree spirit.
I remember rubbing against a boy
in bed one morning, the two of us

joined by his younger sister,
who let us touch her private place —
still hairless, rose-colored

skin folded in the shape
of a little bell. Let us
touch her not with our fingers,

no, but only with an ice cube.
This came back to me many years
later, as I spoke to a woman

at a cocktail party, ice
ringing softly in my glass
and the buckskin fringes

draped around her throat, trembling.
I felt suddenly small, as if
I were some hairy, stooped caveman

who had been quick-frozen
in a freak inversion of arctic air,
as if the raw chunk of woolly mammoth

found clenched in my fist, thawed,
cooked and tasted by archaeologists,
ten thousand years later, was still sweet.

Famous People Hunting and Dancing

Fred Astaire, half-strolling, half-floating
along a tree-lined avenue one afternoon,
leans against a fence that surrounds an asylum
for the mentally ill and notices a peephole
bored into one of its slats. Suddenly a hunter
on the scent of a mystery, he places his eye
against the hole. An eye belonging
to an inmate stares back at him.
Ernest Hemingway, deciphering secret signs
scratched on trees, hunts fleeing SS troops
through the French countryside, while Hitler,
at ease on the terrace of his Bavarian hunting lodge,
winds up a Victrola and dances a stiff little jig,
looking just like the golem brought to life by a cabalist
reciting secret incantations of the Baal Shem Tov.
The inmate staring at Fred Astaire isn't surprised;
hadn't she just seen him in *Top Hat*?
Hadn't she once witnessed the great Nijinsky,
also an inmate, in what many consider
his last dance — a leap, straight up, hands
at his side, expressionless — that the middle-aged,
overweight, catatonic dancer had performed
for a famous photographer?
Even Truman Capote tap dances for nickels
on a riverboat, as Louis Armstrong plays a slow
rendition of "Dixie." Meanwhile, a hunting party
of Negritos find themselves hunted by white strangers,
unaware that the leader of the strangers

is Jack London, that he sailed to their island
on his yacht, *The Snark*, named after a famous poem.
It is night, and the inmate who peeked at Fred Astaire
is flipping through *Mythologies of the Great Hunt*
by a famous scholar. She stares at the pile of naked,
dead Ona tribesmen. They are encircled
by leather-clad hunters whose hands plop over
rifles balanced on their shoulders. Are they
dancing a relaxed, post-hunt, crucifixion dance?
Now she closes her eyes, listens to the whooshing music
of a police helicopter fluttering overhead,
its searchlight illuminating the hiding places.

Nellie's Place

"Straight out of central casting,"
I said to my daughter. "This looks
so much like a truck stop,
it could be in a movie."

Actually she's not my daughter
but looks like she could be.
I've told her so many times about
my chance rendezvous with her mother
one night more than thirty years ago
that I was beginning to believe it myself.

She pretends to cover her ears,
but I think she likes my story
about the be-in at Golden Gate Park,
or the night, at the Fillmore,
I heard Voznesensky shout his poems
in Russian, danced by myself
to the Jefferson Airplane
and got tangled in a haze of pot smoke,
swirling lasers, tie-dyed, billowing silk,
and there, suddenly in my arms
was her mother, looking up at me
like an angel that had just slipped
into this plane of existence —
surprised, amused, slightly outraged,
embarrassed — kind of the way she,
my stepdaughter, looks up at me
when I tell her these stories.

Out of central casting—
Nellie's Place: the grizzled miner,
buck knife in his belt, yuppie fly fishermen
decked out in Orvis; bikers in black leather,
one with silver hair down to his waist
wearing a turquoise and bear-claw necklace;
beer-bellied truckers gathered around
a rack of self-help books.

As we drove off in darkness
I pointed out the rocks
where Captain Kirk
was transported to the cowboy planet,
but I didn't mention my uneasiness
at night in these mountains:
the woman calling Triple A
on her cell phone
when she was mauled
by a mountain lion,
gang graffiti on boulders,
the crew that cleans up sites used
for animal sacrifice,
the new police helicopter,
with its night-vision scope,
and infrared heat-seeking devices,
search parties, vultures.

And who was Nellie? I wondered,
perhaps to cheer myself up,
as we drove on toward Nellie's Peak
and Nellie's Trail. She came here
in 1901, just a waitress
for a few years at Doc Beatty's
Squirrel Inn. Nellie Hawkins . . .
who was she, that she is not forgotten,
that even the wind tumbling
down the valley, even a voice
from the river roiling around
in an old man's sleep
is said to sometimes speak her name?

We drove in silence while I thought of
another story to tell my stepdaughter,
as if I could rearrange the past.
Perhaps I'd combine my Pre-Raphaelite
image of Nellie with her mother —
peasant dress, orange and blowsy
like ranunculus petals; white Mexican blouse;
sandals, of course . . . maybe a campground
or a commune.

After Reading a Recently Declassified Manual
on Interrogation

Now I realize that they switched the numbers
on the motel doors. Back then, I thought
the entire contents of my room had been moved
to another room — and that everything,
even the cigarettes in the ashtray, had been
set up again in exactly the same way.
There was a card on the night table addressed
to me. In childish handwriting it asked, "Are you
still there, Pooh?" Then it answered, "Yes, I am
still here, Piglet." I thought, How nice — everyone
must get a card like this. I noticed that all the clocks,
over the front desk, in the lobbies,
in the lounge, were set at different hours.
Now I understand why, having read the manual.
Even beneath stripes of black marker
I can make out the phrase *Retarding,*
advancing time. If I managed to fall asleep
they woke me with odd questions: *Have you ever*
known anyone with star-shaped irises? Have you ever
received an empty envelope in the mail?
When I tried to give them what I thought
was a good answer, they became angry with me.
My half-hearted cooperation was not rewarded.
But they seemed to approve when I didn't cooperate.
Eventually I felt like I was gently rocking
back and forth on my favorite rocking horse,
wearing my favorite 'jammies, the flannel ones
with spots like a pinto pony. My ten-gallon hat

would slip over my eyes as they questioned me.
While sensors exerted a careful pressure
on my pulse, I began to feel guilty for things
I did not do. I confessed to acts I had been accused of,
wrongfully, when I was a child: feeding an infant
cigarette butts, pulling down a little girl's playsuit,
wearing brass knuckles in the fourth grade.
It was then they began to coax me back, gradually,
toward what the manual calls *full reversal.*
Now I realize they switched the numbers
on the motel doors, not the rooms. The note
was from a lover, a married woman I was seeing
at the time. I don't recall everything I told them,
but I do remember climbing out of a darkness
on a ladder of rationalizations, which they provided.
Phrases were folded into soft music and white noise
while I made up for lost sleep. Reassuring phrases,
such as: *They made you do it. Everyone is doing it.*
You are good, really good at heart.

Note Folded Thirteen Ways

When you speak to me I feel my blood sliding
beneath my skin, and I remember my father.
I see him behind your eyes, as if I stared
into the past through the wrong end of a telescope.
He used to take me to cowboy bars and pass me off
as his girlfriend. I remember Old Spice aftershave,
Hank Williams's "I'm So Lonesome I Could Die," the two
of us slowly turning to that sad, ghostly waltz,
his smiling down at me, the envious glances of strangers.
Later, walking along a tree-lined street in the dark,
I would hold on to his left arm and let my right breast
brush against it with every other step
in a kind of marching rhythm. I wanted him all to myself.
Is that why I once snipped off my sister's braid while she slept?
Why, when he went away, I would take his letters to mother
from the mailbox and hide them under my mattress?
He use to call me his Little Femme Fatale, his Lady in Red.
"What I like best about you," he'd say,
"is that you're like me, capable of betrayal."
I used to fantasize we were sidekicks driving
across the country robbing banks in small towns,
that I would walk into a jail where he was being held,
me all innocent in a gingham dress, Mary Jane shoes,
white stockings, pull a pistol out of a picnic basket
and set him free. I scrawled, "I always desire my teachers,"
on a scrap of paper and slipped it into your notebook.
You will never know who wrote it. Even If you took me
in your arms you would not know because I would disappear,

lifted, completely taken up, enclosed into something large,
warm and feathery. I would be a country road that stretches
into the distance. You would be a dark cloud arched
over a white horizon, ragged at its edges, raining
streaks of black rain that never touch the ground.

Ballad of the Blue Truck

⸻

"You're not an Indian, are you?"
was what I heard from desk clerks
in Arizona. "What in the hell
is this truck?" was what the Highway
Patrol wanted to know each time they
pulled me over in six Western states.
"Powell Plymouth, officer — handmade,
piece by piece, assembled in a junkyard
by a man named Powell."
                              Body made
of fiberboard, hood held down
by four snaps attached to rubber bands.
When a semi passed, it would flap, caught
in the suction, frantic, like a pterodactyl
coming to life, bellow, lift off and take flight,
sailing over the cab to crash-land in a clump
about fifty yards behind me.
                              No key,
ignition was the light switch pulled
halfway out and twisted just so. Its throttle
was held into a socket with string, and Powell
had signed each creation, engraving his name
in one of the many secret compartments.

It was painted with flat, sky-blue house paint
the same color as the robes of *La Virgen
de Guadalupe*, whose postcard I had taped
over the driver's seat. She stood, hands folded

in prayer, on a crescent moon under the ocean;
the striped, 3-D fish flashing around her head
were stars.

Was it she who alerted my guardian angel
that night fifty miles from Phoenix, when I
missed a curve, shot down a hillside,
and plowed through an apple orchard?
I kept going through a gauntlet of outraged
trees that threw branches, banged the hood,
windshield, and scraped the fenders.
Was it she, days later, who directed
my hungry attention to the truck bed
brimful with slightly tart, sweet apples?

Finally my truck was taken away, towed
by police. Then they gutted it and sold
its parts for scrap, wrapped its body
in chains like a gangster and sent it to sleep
in the ocean of towed cars. Fish swim around
it now, through it, in and out the windows,
wondering, What kind of creature would live
in this odd blue shell?
                         Blue truck, your radiator
and tailpipes were welded into a metal man
that stands like a scarecrow outside a body shop
in Last Chance, Idaho. One rusty, flute-like
arm is raised in a gesture of greeting. The other

holds a banjo made of a hubcap and wire.
A muffler is his face, three bullet holes
his eyes and mouth. A steering wheel is his hat,
blackbirds and magpies his epaulets. He seems
to be staring at the sky.

Koh-i-Noor

—⁓—

It was years ago that I dreamt of a silver-haired
warrior, old, weary of dragging his bones into battle
buckled in armor like a cockroach. I probably got him
from a film, *Alexander Nevsky* — the Templars
in their white robes and black, bucket-shaped helmets,
sinking slowly beneath an ice field as it broke up
to the music of Prokofiev. I knew the warrior
was plotting some escape, a turning to the other side,
but could trust no one, especially his servant,
an Igor type who dragged one foot. It wasn't from a movie
that I got Igor. Igor was Julie, an old man from Latvia
who washed dishes with me on my first job.
A former Cossack, he was fond of lunging
with a mop, stomping one boot down on tile and
giving out a yell — the mop suddenly becoming a lance
shoved into an underbelly of horse. Sometimes
he would bring a scrapbook to work and pull
a crumpled picture from it — two dead men, each
with a penis and a pipe stuffed into their mouths.
He would gesture with his fingers to show
how pipe and penis formed a tilted cross and say to me
with a smile, "Woman, it was woman troops do this."
I became that old warrior betrayed by his servant.
I rose, strapped to a death machine, a sort of Ferris wheel
that carried me up. When I saw, across the river, back-lit
battlements of the enemy I felt an incredible happiness
and began to repeat the word "Koh-i-Noor." This came from
the brand name of a notebook I had. "Koh-i-Noor"

was printed across its cover, and beneath it, in parentheses,
a translation from Persian, "Mountain of Light."
My servant didn't even wait for me to die,
just turned and walked away. But as he turned,
he disappeared, and a young woman stepped out of him.
Like throwing off old clothes she stepped out of him
and he was gone. All she had of him was his limp.
I don't know where she came from, but I have
seen her often. As she made her way toward the river,
she stopped, turned to look up at me, and I saw
that this time her eyes were an unearthly blue — bluer
than the light trapped inside an iceberg for a thousand years.

Descent

A man is wandering
through the outskirts of Hell,
that is to say, insomnia.
He's even tried reading Dante,
but all that did was remind him
of when he was lost on a day hike:
the crumbling incline,
too late, too far to go back —
sidestepping down a wadi
as if into a construction site
or an open-pit mine.
The dramatic way some stars
were framed in precarious archways
didn't comfort, nor did
the bizarre skull faces of caves.
He could hear the soft voices
of Bedouin sheepherders
down below, and he stepped
on each stone like a ghost.
Just as he recalls how he found
a burlap sack to keep him warm,
wild grapes and water dripping
from granite, he falls asleep.
But his sleep is a spiral staircase
he descends even as he hears
something not quite human
ascending. Slowly, faint at first,
snorting, step by step, its feet

dragging until they stand face to face.
What a disappointing minotaur.
Not hairy or smelly, not like Picasso's.
And such a strange color, something
between eraser and international
safety orange, head more praying mantis
than bull. So what if it stares with eyes
blank as buttons — the man is no
Theseus. Looking down
he sees that he hasn't any legs,
and his hands are indistinct.
He puts them together and they blend
into a blur of wings, as if he held
a fluttering pigeon. The creature
also looks disappointed.
He had expected a young woman
wearing a linen smock, carrying a candle.
They both pause, then without a shrug
or a nod, proceed, one down into darkness,
the other up toward what may be morning.

Naked City

—⁓—

She was the kind of gal who would look elegant
even if she was wearing nothing but handcuffs.
She had a way of leaning against a wall in an alley
that made you think she was wearing a gold lamé
evening gown, balancing an onyx cigarette holder
on her fingertips while a diamond bracelet
flashed from her wrist. When she sat on a bench
in the station house, doing her nails, humming
to herself, I said a silent prayer that she would not
raise her skirt to adjust her stockings. If she did
I'd have to think about baseball, which I despise,
or the locations of seemingly unrelated homicides
forming a crude calligraphy of her name on a map.
By now you've guessed that I was nothing to her,
an omniscient, voice-over narrator watching her sashay
in and out of trouble in a hundred different locations.
And what was that stupid tune she always hummed?
It was, "one-two-three the conga," the same one I found
myself humming after I brought her in for questioning
and got nowhere. It was "one-two-three the conga," stuck
in my head as I stood in the interrogation room, alone,
rubbing lipstick from her Styrofoam cup against my lips.
So I thought I could latch on to the small waist of happiness
and follow it anywhere, but pursuing happiness
is like pursuing a murderer — it has its depressing moments.

Their Words

He was fond of saying
"machete" at the most
inopportune moments;
for instance, while
they took a bath together
and he sat behind her,
his legs wrapped
around her hips,
soaping her back
with oatmeal soap
he'd whisper in her
ear, "machete."

She called him
"My Little Escarpment."
He didn't know what
she meant by that.
Was it something muscular
and slimy, like escargot?
Or did she think he
was her balustrade,
someone she could lean from
and wave to a passing crowd,
someone she could leap over,
or climb up on with a rose
clenched between her teeth?

If he was really in a good mood
and she asked him to work
in the garden, maybe
trim the rose bushes
he'd say, "Get the machete."
He liked the sound of *g*
slashing through the *e*'s
and knocking against the *t*'s.

"Let's have a daughter," he'd say,
"and name her Machete."
He imagined an
eleven-year-old girl
boys were afraid of.
Machete, willowly blonde
with a pony tail, sweet,
sensitive Machete, but stern
with an eleven-year-old's
sense of justice, and a tiny,
crescent-shaped
fencing scar on her cheek.

Once he spent several nights
crying out in his sleep
in what seemed to be an ancient
Middle Eastern language,
perhaps Babylonian.
It was during this episode

that he sat suddenly upright,
in a cold sweat, clutched his chest
and whispered, "Nunishmu, poison
arrows of darkness have got me!"

Her highest exclamation was not
words at all but a low,
teeth-clenched, sputtering growl.
That's when he knew
she was truly happy.
He'd feel as if
he were floating,
carried along under stars
in the narrowing circumference
of a vast whirlpool.

Toward the Blue Peninsula

You find the hotel room painfully white. Everything — the walls, the fleecy carpet, alabaster busts on marble pedestals, the gown hanging in the closet — is white.

Outside the window clouds rush by — opulent, nineteenth-century clouds, bedecked, bewigged, wearing capes and scarves and making sublime nineteenth-century gestures.

The room has a hole in the plaster. You stare into it, hoping to see the beautiful woman next door as she dries herself after a bath. She spoke to you in the hallway, telling you about her boyfriend, the famous poet. She showed you a sketch he drew — her sleeping face and all around it, on her pillow, tiny knights, castles, dragons, and towers.

She was standing in the hallway when she showed you the sketch. She invited you in. You did not accept. That was thirty-nine years ago. Now you have invented this hotel you wander through. You are not actually a guest, but the door to one of the rooms was unlocked so you entered.

Was there a bird in the room that escaped from its open cage through the window? Is that why you find a small white feather on the floor?

Not Joan Baez

I'm sitting on top of Marty's dryer
in his porch that looms over backyards
like the prow of a freighter pounding through waves
and fog, and it's as if I'm standing at the railing looking
at you, kid, through a mist of years. The collar of my leather
jacket is up, a Bogart cigarette dangles from my lips
and you don't know it yet but someday you're going
to see me here, catch your breath and get that sinking,
slightly woozy feeling, the same falling sadness in the belly
I'll feel when I see you in the picture you took of yourself
back in your art school days.

You, Beautiful — naked, wrist against your forehead
covering your eyes so arty, and where your belly should be
just a clean round hole, no blood, no gore, just a hole
revealing the slats of a suburban deck
both inside and outside of you in perfect alignment:
doctor's wife angst, something missing, a hole that can't be filled,
even if you were a sculpture by Henry Moore, even if your waist
were curvaceous granite with a river pouring through it.

I'll felt cheated, my one chance to see you naked
back in the days when you were a Joan Baez look-alike
and I was a motorcycle tough of the James Dean persuasion,
but instead all I get is this seventies darkroom surrealism,
my future wife, the napkin ring.

Let's fast forward about twenty-five years
to one of those perfect tourist days in New York:
it's fall, sunny, and as we're crossing the street
into Central Park a character driving a hansom cab
pulls his horse up short, stares down at you,
and nods, saying, "I know, I know,
you're not really Joan Baez, not Joan Baez."

No, you're not, but memory has gotten mixed up
with desire, and I am beginning to think that you were
that girl who held my books on a bus when I was too shy
to get your phone number; that you were the one
who snuck up on me while I was asleep in Marty's yard,
the one he said climbed the fence, then leaned over me,
holding her long black hair out with her hands
but its tips brushed my face anyway and suddenly
I thought the sun was smiling, raining down large, warm,
friendly drops of light; that it was you waving
from a window over the backyard when Marty pointed
and said, "There she is." And here you are on the deck
of a freighter standing across from me. We disembark tomorrow,
but for now it's warm and starry, we're looking at each other,
and although we haven't spoken yet, I have a feeling
this is one of those nights when everything is possible.

Presences

The red-headed cop who held a gun to my head,
an old man I mistook for an angel,
the lawyer who materialized at my side
just as I was about to be sentenced to two years
at Rikers, who got me off with ten days then turned
and disappeared in the crowd — they come together here,
along with a punch-drunk fighter
from the farm labor camp and Louise from the bed
across from mine when I had my tonsils out.

I first saw the old man taking shape, approaching
me along a desert road where I was walking,
alone, not much money, no jacket,
and no place to stay. We met, sat on a boulder,
talked a bit, shared my last cigarette, then walked off
in opposite directions, but not before he touched my face,
looked into my eyes and said, "No harm shall come to you."
Today, the red-headed cop slaps me on the back, says,
"How've you been Mr. Houdini, Mr. Monkey?
Squirm and scamper your way out of any jails lately?"

Louise, the girl from the hospital, becomes Louise,
the clerk in a clothing shop in Edinburgh, just as
the itinerant scissors-sharpener, a diminutive old fellow
with a rakish tilt to his tweed hat, took a stone out of his pouch
and stroked it up and down the scissors, and I knew that standing
next to Louise was the best part of his day and that Louise
did not really need her scissors sharpened. I felt something,

a presence, as if a door opened and someone could see us
by looking through Louise's eyes, the way I felt like a presence
staring into a doll's house in a craft museum.

Not a house, but a miniature general store
with a cracker barrel, shelves lined with canned goods,
bolts of cloth, boxes of hard candy, whiskey bottles,
and a rack of John B. Stetson hats. But even better
was a stairway up the back of the building
that led to a room. Striped wallpaper, lace on the window,
a brass bed, a white pitcher and bowl on a marble-topped
basin, leather shaving strop hanging from a wooden peg.
Sometimes I have found myself there, climbing the stairs,
thinking, the old man was right about the room.
Down in the store, the lawyer, whose hair is now red,
is working as a clerk. He smiles to himself, as he
removes a Room-for-Rent sign from the window.

Journal of the Lost Years

Asleep on a cot in the basement, I was awakened
by a loud bang, like the sound of magma
breaking through crusted earth.
Two ghosts drifted through the room,
but they were enveloped in conversation
and didn't seem to notice me. And then
I was standing on the edge of a precipice
with a pelt wrapped around my shoulders,
while two women, both blonde and muscular,
cast menacing glances in my direction.
I noticed how the color of their faces
lacked gradation. That's the way it is,
I thought, when dolls are disguised as humans.
To distract them until I could slip away
I offered them my mantle,
my transparent second skin, impenetrable
yet so delicate it could catch sunlight
and hold it captive and glowing in its lacy net,
offered them my mantle like Elijah to Elisha —
my mantle, this achievement that enfolds
and protects. They helped me peel it
from by body with trembling hands and long,
sharp fingernails. Then I was back in the basement,
exhausted, my pulse flickering, and pronouncing
myself legally dead, I knelt over the green, filmy
scum of a pond that had formed on the floor
in my absence. I knelt, not in prayer but more like
a bird of prey in a cage hunched over a sinewy scrap.

The two Nordic goddesses, beautiful, though
not my type, drifted away with the ghosts.
Perhaps they were also ghosts. Perhaps
eternity was just a late Sunday afternoon
in the park as far as they were concerned —
a painting by Seurat, everything shimmering,
barely held together by illusion.

ACKNOWLEDGMENTS

Some of the poems in this collection have appeared in the following magazines and anthologies, sometimes in slightly different form and some with different titles.

Art Life: "Toward the Blue Peninsula"

Bloomsbury Review: "A Diver for the NYPD Talks to His Girlfriend"

Blue Mesa Review: "Elite Syncopations," "To My Ex-Husband"

Colorado Review: "Ballad of the Blue Truck," "Cat's Cradle," "The Laws of Salvage"

Crab Orchard Review: "Legends of the West," "Birdlike Sonata"

Crania: "Confessions of an Exhibitionist," "Rancho Notorious," "Intimations of Ratoon"

Dominion Review: "The Ceremony," "The Palazzo"

Georgetown Review: "Descent," "Paducah"

Greensboro Review: "The Detective and the Curio," "Note Folded Thirteen Ways"

Luna: "After Reading a Recently Declassified Manual on Interrogation," "Nellie's Place"

Mid-American Review: "Vernon"

Mosaic: "Shark," "Wasted Lives"

Mudfish: "Koh-i-Nor," "Star Chamber," "His Wife, Folded"

Ploughshares: "Certain Images, Excluded from My Poems, Form a Parade"

Prairie Schooner: "A Death in Larkspur Canyon," "What Passes for Sleep"

Printed Matter: "Famous People Hunting and Dancing"

The Prose Poem: "Just Like Saint Peter," "His Wife, Folded"

"Just Like Saint Peter" appears in *The Best of The Prose Poem*, ed. Peter Johnson (Providence College), 2000; "A Diver for the NYPD Talks to His Girlfriend" and "A Death in Larkspur Canyon" appear in *Urban Nature*, ed. Laure-Anne Bosselaar (Milkweed Editions, 2000); "Nobody Here But Us" appears in *Outsiders*, ed. Laure-Ann Bosselaar (Milkweed Editions, 1999); "Dangerous Hats," "A Diver for the NYPD Talks to His Girlfriend," "Elite Syncopations," "El Zapato," "Nobody Here but Us," and

"Note Folded Thirteen Ways" appear in *Touching the Fire: Fourteen Poets of the Latino Renaissance*, ed. Ray Gonzalez (Doubleday, 1998); "Note Folded Thirteen Ways" appears in *The 1997 Pushcart Prize XXI: Best of the Small Presses*, ed. Bill Henderson (Pushcart Press, 1996); "Legends of the West" and "Note Folded Thirteen Ways" appear in *Fishtrap Anthology.*

I would also like to gratefully acknowledge the following organizations and presses for recognizing some of the poems in this collection with awards: "Note Folded Thirteen Ways," the 1997 Pushcart Prize, and the 1995 Greensboro Award, *Greensboro Review*; "Against Frog" and "His Wife, Folded," 1997 Poetry in the Windows Prize, Arroyo Arts Collective; "Star Chamber," 1997 Mudfish Prize, *Mudfish*; and "Descent" and "Paducah," 1997 Georgetown Poetry Prize, *Georgetown Review*. Thanks also to the California Arts Council for its generous support.

Richard Garcia was born in San Francisco in 1941. His father was from Puerto Rico and his mother from Mexico. His previous book of poetry, *The Flying Garcias*, was published by the University of Pittsburgh Press in 1993. In 1994 he received an MFA in creative writing from Warren Wilson College. He has won many awards for his work, including a Pushcart Prize, the Cohen Award from *Ploughshares*, the *Georgetown Review* Poetry Prize, the Greensboro Award from the *Greensboro Review*, and the Mudfish Award from *Mudfish*. He has received a fellowship from the National Endowment for the Arts and a fellowship from the California Arts Council, which also awarded him three Artist-in-Residence grants for his work as Poet-in-Residence at the Long Beach Museum of Art. Since 1991 he has been the Poet-in-Residence at Children's Hospital Los Angeles, where, with the assistance of a series of grants from the California Arts Council and the Johnny Mercer Foundation, he conducts poetry and art workshops for hospitalized children.

BOA EDITIONS, LTD.:

American Poets Continuum Series

COLOPHON

The publication of this book was made possible,
in part, by the special support of the following individuals:

Dane & Judy Gordon, Richard Garth & Mimi Hwang,
Deb & Kip Hale, Robert & Willy Hursh,
Boo Poulin, Allen & Suzy Spencer,
Judith Taylor, Pat & Michael Wilder.

———∿∿∿———

This book was set in Californian and Goudy Village fonts,
both based on the type designs of Frederic Goudy,
by Valerie Brewster, Scribe Typography.

The cover was designed by Lisa Mauro / Mauro Design,
Rochester, New York.

Manufacturing was by McNaughton & Gunn,
Saline, Michigan.